Horseshoe Crabs and Shorebirds

The Story of a Food Web

By Victoria Crenson

Illustrated by Annie Cannon

Marshall Cavendish New York

To Jeff —*V.C.*

To Limulus: ancient, strange, and part of us —*A.C.*

Marshall Cavendish, 99 White Plains Road, Tarrytown, NY 10591
www.marshallcavendish.com

Library of Congress Cataloging-in-Publication Data

Crenson, Victoria.
Horseshoe crabs and shorebirds: the story of a food web / by Victoria Crenson ; illustrations by Annie
Cannon.— 1st
ed.
    p. cm.
Summary: Presents a portrait of the Delaware Bay in the spring when a wide variety of animals, includ-
ing minnows, mice, turtles, raccoons, and especially migrating shorebirds, come to feed on the billions
of eggs laid by horseshoe crabs.
 ISBN 0-7614-5115-3
 1. Limulus polyphemus—Eggs—Delaware Bay (Del. and N.J.)—Juvenile literature. 2. Food chains
(Ecology)—Delaware Bay (Del. and N.J.)—Juvenile literature. [1. Horsehoe crabs—Eggs. 2. Food chains
(Ecology)—Delaware Bay (Del. and N.J.) 3. Ecology—Delaware Bay (Del. and N.J.) 4. Delaware Bay
(Del. and N.J.)] 1. Cannon, Annie, ill. II.
Title.
 QL447.7.C74 2003
 577'.16—dc21   2002156473

The text of this book is set in Berkeley.
The illustrations are rendered in watercolor.
Book design by Virginia Pope

Printed in China
First edition
6 5 4 3 2

Author's Note

Although horseshoe crabs are seen along the Atlantic coast from Maine
to Mexico, most of them live in Delaware Bay. A large number of migrating
shorebirds in the Western Hemisphere stop to refuel on horseshoe crab eggs.
They depend on the superabundance of this unique food source. That is why
many people are alarmed at the sharp drop in the number of horseshoe crabs.
Some blame the fishermen who gather thousands of horseshoe crabs as the
creatures come ashore to lay eggs, then cut them up to sell as eel bait. Others
say building vacation homes and bulkheads has robbed horseshoe crabs of
nesting beaches. With fewer horseshoe crabs returning to nest each spring,
fewer shorebirds are being counted during their northward migrations. If
something is not done soon to protect horseshoe crabs, the millions of creatures that depend upon this ancient food web may perish. The great egg feast,
one of nature's most dramatic spring events, could become a thing of the past.

—*Victoria Crenson*

It is a foggy-drizzle night in early spring. Deep down in the cold muck at the bottom of Delaware Bay, ancient-looking creatures begin a journey.

They are horseshoe crabs—descendants of seagoing spiders. Each spring they crawl from the bay bottom and travel to sandy beaches to dig nests and lay billions of eggs. Horseshoe crabs have been making this journey every spring since before the time of the dinosaurs. Upon the bounty of their pearly green eggs, a remarkable food web has grown.

Horseshoe crabs travel slowly and at night. Walking on ten spidery legs, protected by hard, bowl-shaped shells, they plow through the mud, stirring up worms, clams, and dead fish to eat. Bristles on their legs grind up the food as they walk. Behind their legs, stacked up like pages of a book, are flat gills for breathing. When it suits them, horseshoe crabs turn upside down and swim. They flap the "pages" of their book gills like paddles and use long, spiky tails as steering rudders. Each night's travel brings them a little closer to shore.

Meanwhile, far away at the tip of South America, millions of shorebirds begin a journey of their own. In spring many flocks fly halfway around the world to their nesting grounds near the Arctic Circle. During the long and exhausting flight, shorebirds stop only a few times to rest and feed. The hungry birds must find plenty of food at annual stopover spots or they will not have the energy to go on. Flapping their wings constantly day and night, they head northward toward Delaware Bay. They must arrive in time for the great horse-shoe crab egg feast and refuel, or they will never reach the Arctic to nest.

On a warm evening in May at Delaware Bay, after many nights' journey, an army of brown domes emerges from the water and gathers along the shoreline. Row upon row, for miles along the beach, male horseshoe crabs assemble.

The high tide churns, whirls, sucks foamy suds around them. Shells *clack-clack* together as waves shove them back and forth. Dark tails poke up out of the water like waving spears.

A few horseshoe crabs get flipped onto
their backs. Legs kicking the air,
they are sent sliding up the
sand or cartwheeling help-
lessly through the surf.

But most of the males do not break ranks and venture
ashore. They fight the tide, hold the line, and wait for hours
for the females to arrive.

A full moon peers over the lip of the horizon and spills silver light on thousands of dark, glistening shells. The tide has turned. The wait is finally over—females ride the waves to shore.

Quickly the males crowd around them. They use special clasper claws on their front legs to hook onto the back edges of the females' shells. Females are bigger and stronger than males. Each tows a male up onto the beach—*scoot, rest, scoot, rest*—up to the tide line, where she settles into the wet sand and begins to dig her nest.

The female pushes deep into the sand with the front of her shell until she is almost covered. *Scritch, scrape*, she digs with her legs. When a shallow nest is finished, a small purse covering her book gills opens and out fall thousands of pearly green eggs. The male fertilizes the eggs with sperm before he is dragged to the next nest.

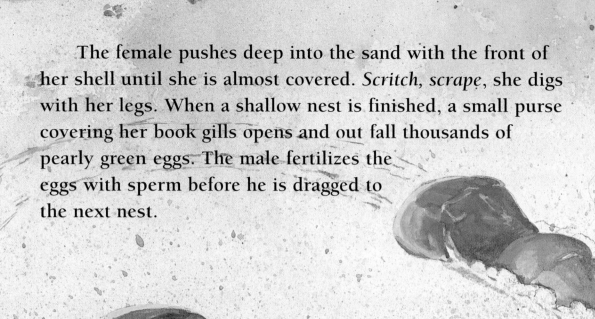

Females dig several nests and drop clutches of eggs in each. Then, with the male tagalongs still in tow, the females head back to the water. They leave looping figure-eight drag trails behind them like signatures in the sand. Each night for several weeks, horseshoe crabs return to lay more and more eggs.

Hundreds of thousands of horseshoe crabs. Billions of eggs.

Many eggs are swept out of the nests and sucked into the receding waves. By morning, floating eggs wash up on the shell-speckled beach. They collect along the tide line like a broad, green-beaded hem on the bay's ruffled skirt.

On the beach, in the water or under the sand lie billions of green eggs.

Now the great egg feast begins.

The first
to arrive is a
blackbird with a
scarlet patch on its
shoulder. It struts down
the beach, stopping every few sec-
onds to gobble up green eggs. Each egg
is only a tiny mouthful, but together the
eggs add up to a bird's banquet. The blackbird fills its gullet
and then flies off to its nest in the tall reeds of a nearby
marsh to feed its hungry nestlings.

Next come a couple of fat mourning doves and a grackle with shiny blue-black feathers. The birds daintily *peck-peck* among the pebbles at the water's edge, being careful not to get their feet wet. All of a sudden, in a blur of wings, a horde of noisy laughing gulls flies in and, with crazy cries, chases the other birds off the beach.

The gulls crowd together, backs to the sun. Their black heads bob up and down in unison as they jab at the wet sand and gorge themselves on horseshoe crab eggs.

The biggest horde of feasters finally arrives. Flying almost nonstop from their winter homes many thousands of miles to the south, from remote beaches in Patagonia and Tierra del Fuego, more than a million starving shorebirds reach Delaware Bay—just in time for the great egg feast!

Red knots and ruddy turnstones, sanderlings and plovers,
joined by dowitchers and dunlins, willets and yellowlegs, all
arrive hungry and eager to dine on salty-sweet eggs.
    With shrill squeals and whistles, flock after flock descends.
They swoop, swirl, swarm over the flat beaches and begin
to feast.

Long-billed dowitchers poke and
root beneath the wet sand at the
water's edge. Yellowlegs wade in
the shallows, slurping up egg after
egg. Sandpipers pick up eggs while playing
group tag with the gentle waves. Turnstones
scoop out deep holes in crab nests and suck up
fresh eggs like so many miniature green peas.
When sanderlings try to horn in on a good hole, there is a
noisy squabble. Gangs of gulls roam the beach and bully the
other shorebirds into giving way.

Crowded into the small strip
of tide flat between dunes and surf
is one of the largest bird gatherings
on earth. A million birds feast and
feud and fill the air with their loud
calls. All day long, soft brown and
white feathers bounce down the beach
on a steady bay breeze.

High in the sky,
riding the breeze on its
long pointed wings, a
young peregrine falcon spies
a feast of birds spread out
on the beach below. It soars
silently along the shoreline,
watching and waiting.

A small flock of sandpipers, startled by some gulls, rises from the sand like a cloud and moves out over the water. The birds fly in tight formation. As they turn toward shore, they flash the whites of their underwings. Quick as lightning, the falcon drops from the sky and speeds into the flock. Its sharp talons grab a sandpiper from the air. The falcon gives its prey a squeeze, and the little bird goes limp. Lazily the falcon flies inland—flap, flap, glide—to its perch on an old water tower, where it can rest and feed. It will return often to the great egg feast.

In shallows just offshore, other
feasters are busy. Large schools of minnows nibble
on floating masses of horseshoe crab eggs. Swimming among
them are visitors from deeper waters—eels and young logger-
head turtles—lured in by the tasty feast of eggs.

Storm clouds roll in from the west and bring a day of rain. As the gray sky deepens to charcoal, the shorebirds retreat to their nighttime roosting spots in the marsh. Meanwhile, the horseshoe crabs crawl ashore as they have each night since the full moon. Raindrops drum with a hollow *tap-tap* on their shells. Some of the large females' shells are encrusted with other animals—mussels, barnacles, and limpets. They look like parade floats as they drag their mates up onto the sand and dig more nests. The rough storm surf tumbles many onto their backs and pushes them high up the beach.

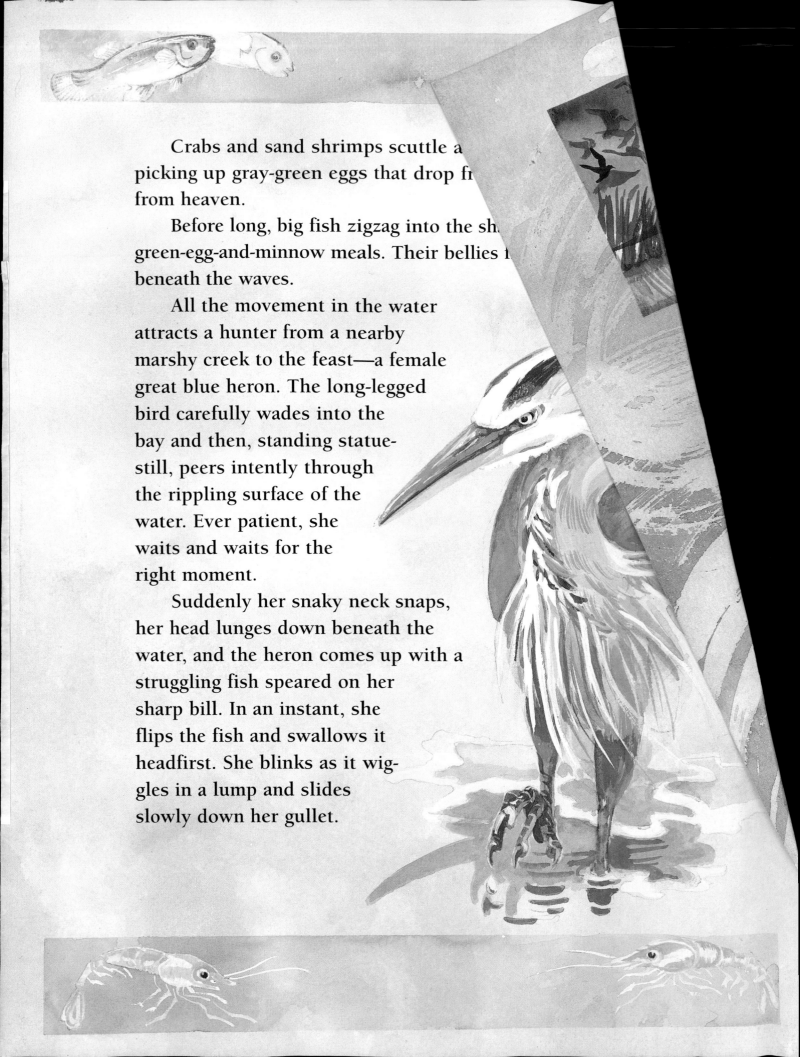

Crabs and sand shrimps scuttle a[bout]
picking up gray-green eggs that drop fr[om]
from heaven.

Before long, big fish zigzag into the sh[allows]
green-egg-and-minnow meals. Their bellies [flash]
beneath the waves.

All the movement in the water
attracts a hunter from a nearby
marshy creek to the feast—a female
great blue heron. The long-legged
bird carefully wades into the
bay and then, standing statue-
still, peers intently through
the rippling surface of the
water. Ever patient, she
waits and waits for the
right moment.

Suddenly her snaky neck snaps,
her head lunges down beneath the
water, and the heron comes up with a
struggling fish speared on her
sharp bill. In an instant, she
flips the fish and swallows it
headfirst. She blinks as it wiggles in a lump and slides
slowly down her gullet.

Crabs and sand shrimps scuttle about on the bottom, picking up gray-green eggs that drop from above like manna from heaven.

Before long, big fish zigzag into the shallows, hunting for green-egg-and-minnow meals. Their bellies flash quicksilver beneath the waves.

All the movement in the water attracts a hunter from a nearby marshy creek to the feast—a female great blue heron. The long-legged bird carefully wades into the bay and then, standing statue-still, peers intently through the rippling surface of the water. Ever patient, she waits and waits for the right moment.

Suddenly her snaky neck snaps, her head lunges down beneath the water, and the heron comes up with a struggling fish speared on her sharp bill. In an instant, she flips the fish and swallows it headfirst. She blinks as it wiggles in a lump and slides slowly down her gullet.

Storm clouds roll in from the west and bring a day of rain. As the gray sky deepens to charcoal, the shorebirds retreat to their nighttime roosting spots in the marsh. Meanwhile, the horseshoe crabs crawl ashore as they have each night since the full moon. Raindrops drum with a hollow *tap-tap* on their shells. Some of the large females' shells are encrusted with other animals—mussels, barnacles, and limpets. They look like parade floats as they drag their mates up onto the sand and dig more nests. The rough storm surf tumbles many onto their backs and pushes them high up the beach.

Just before midnight, the rain stops and, one by one, stars appear. A tiny field mouse skitters down a dune and climbs a mound of sand near the tide line. Its whiskers quiver as it pauses to listen to a faint scraping sound coming from somewhere beneath its feet.

The mound of sand moves as the buried horseshoe crab plows deeper. She stirs up a nest dug there the previous night, and clusters of hidden eggs are tossed up onto the sand in easy reach of the lucky mouse. It stuffs the eggs into its mouth and then skitters back up the dune.

It is late morning and along the high tide line, among the driftwood and debris, are the smelly remains of stranded horseshoe crabs upturned the night before, now baking in the sun. Gulls, never ones to be picky eaters, have already snacked on some of them. Flies buzz about the empty brown bowls. Many more horseshoe crabs lie strewn about the beach, still struggling to right themselves. If the sun dries out their book gills, they will die soon.

Crowds of hungry red knots and sanderlings, intent on foraging for more eggs, mill about the horseshoe crabs as if they are not there. The sandy beach is covered in crisscrossing bird tracks and paw prints from last night's egg feasters— a family of raccoons, a fox . . . and a mouse.

At noontime, two excited boys run down to the water's edge to play. Their loud whoops and cries frighten the shorebirds. With a whoosh of wings, the flocks rise up and regroup farther down the beach, away from the commotion. The boys play a game called rescue-the-horseshoe-crab, and spend hours turning over the creatures to watch them crawl back to the water and disappear into the waves.

Every day from dawn to dusk, the shorebirds have gobbled up horseshoe crab eggs. Now, thanks to the great egg feast, they are strong and fat. Swirling whirlpools of noisy birds spiral about the tidal flats. Like the horseshoe crabs, these migratory birds must travel to their breeding grounds, make nests, and lay eggs. Flocks are already leaving Delaware Bay to head north to the Arctic. Those that get there first will have the best nesting sites for raising their young during the short Arctic summer.

On this sunny, sparkling morning two weeks after their
arrival, as if of one mind, flock by flock, they circle
the flats a few times and then swiftly fly away.
Songbirds and shorebirds, minnows and eels,
turtles and foxes, mice and raccoons, fishes and
shrimps and crabs—the guests at the great egg
feast have eaten more than seven billion eggs. But
many, many horseshoe crab eggs still remain safe in
their nests.

A cool breeze softly shushes through the dune grasses
on a bright moonlit night. Beneath the sand where waves
lick at high tide's edge, a tiny egg is hatching. Out pops
a pale horseshoe crab larva barely the size of a freck-
le. It kicks its five sets of legs and tries to swim
through the wet sand. Wave after wave reaches high
up the beach until finally sand and larva are swept into
the bay along with millions of other horseshoe crab larvae
hatched this night.

In the bay waters, the horseshoe crab larva grows and grows. It sheds old shells and grows larger ones many times until, after eight or ten years, it is finally an adult.

Then one night in early spring, the horseshoe crab crawls from the muck at the bottom of Delaware Bay and begins a journey—a journey horseshoe crabs have been making every spring for millions and millions of years.

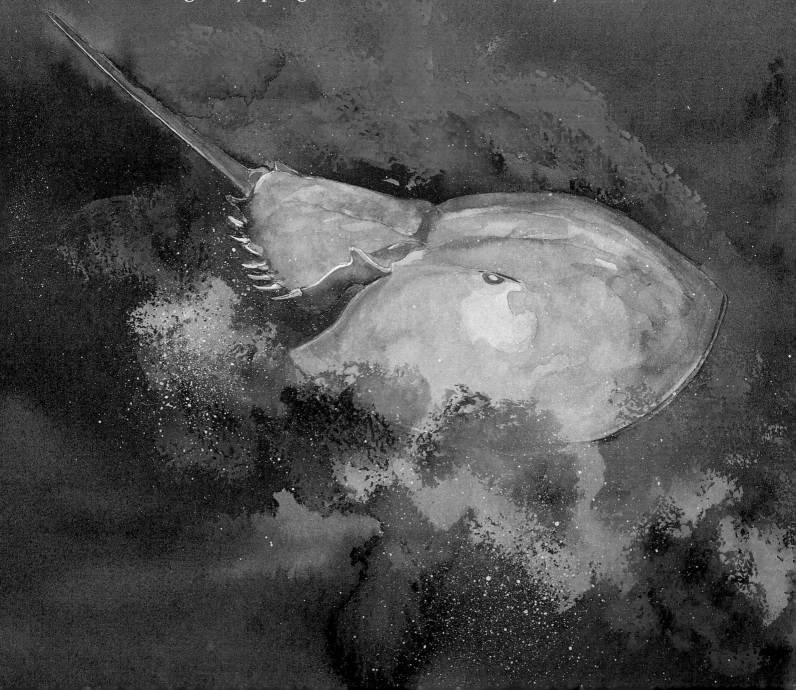

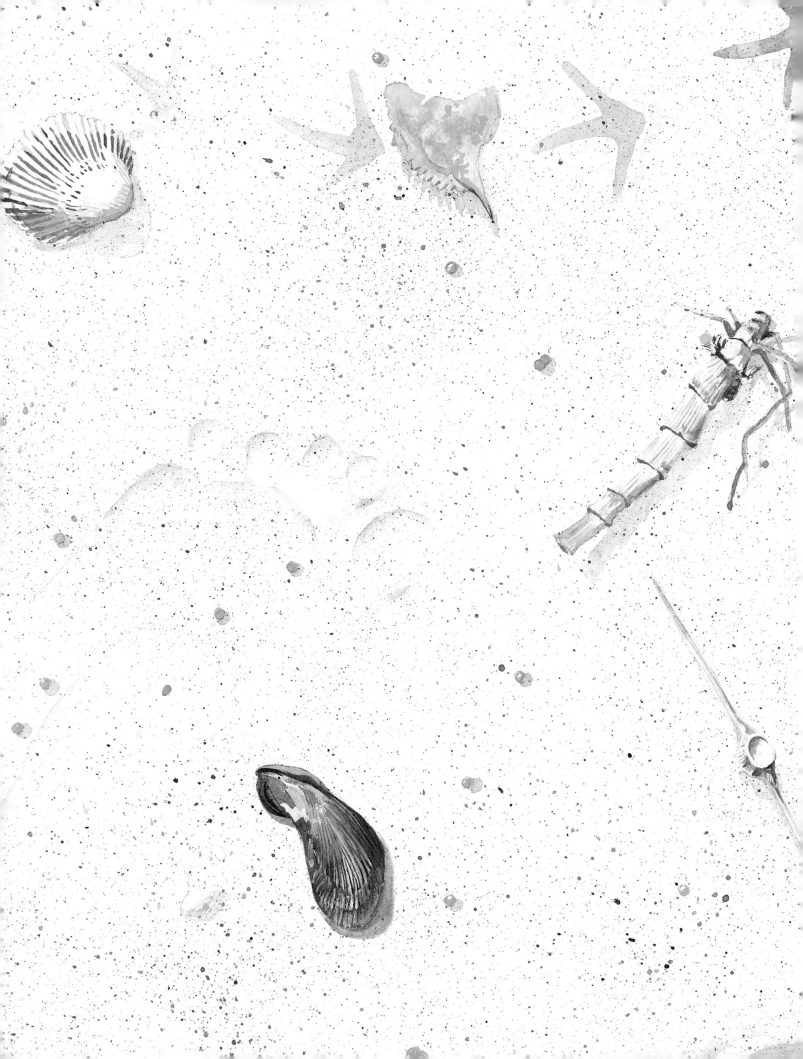